You
Are
Kind

Written By : Jessica Heins
Illustrated By : Pinki Basak

*This book is inspired by my two wonderful moms.
You have guided, loved, supported, and encouraged
me to be who I am, always. I am so grateful for you
and your love each and every day.
Thank you, Thank you, Thank you*

YOU ARE KIND…
You are KIND, here's how we know…
Say it 1 time and then again until you
feel it in your soul!

I am KIND
I am KIND
More ways each day!

I am KIND
I am KIND
YES, I AM!

Say it fast, say it s l o w
I am KIND
I am K I N D
More ways each day!

I am KIND
I am K I N D
YES, I AM!

Say it quiet, say it LOUD
I am kind
I AM KIND
More ways each day!

I am kind
I AM KIND
YES, I AM!

Say it with a smile and feel
your HEARTgrow
I am KIND
I am KIND
More ways each day!

I am KIND
I am KIND
YES, I AM!

Say it while you sit and say it
when you stand
I am KIND
I am KIND
More ways each day!

I am KIND
I am KIND
YES, I AM!

Say it with your eyes closed
I am KIND
I am KIND
More ways each day!

I am KIND
I am KIND
YES, I AM!

Now say it with your heart,
really feel it in your soul
I am kind
I am kind
More each day!

I am KIND
I am KIND
YES, I AM!

"Kindness" is a powerful force that can have a positive ripple effect on both ourselves and others. It starts with being kind to ourselves, as self-compassion lays the foundation for being kind to others. When we show kindness to ourselves, we nurture self-love and self-worth. Taking care of our physical and emotional needs, acknowledging our accomplishments, and being forgiving of our mistakes are all ways we can practice self-kindness.

Kindness is contagious. When we share kindness with others, we create a chain reaction of positivity and compassion. A simple smile, a warm greeting, or a thoughtful gesture can brighten someone's day and even inspire them to pass on kindness to others.

Acts of kindness don't have to be grand gestures; even the smallest acts can make a significant difference. Whether it's writing a kind note, lending a helping hand, or simply listening to someone who needs to talk, each act of kindness contributes to making the world a better place. So, let's make it a habit to be kind to ourselves and others every day. The world can always use more kindness, and it starts with each one of us. Give yourself that hug and spread kindness wherever you go!

THANK YOU!

* 9 7 8 9 6 9 3 6 9 2 3 0 3 *